Samoyeds

Paige V. Polinsky

Checkerboard Library

An Imprint of Abdo Publishing
abdopublishing.com

abdopublishing.com

Published by Abdo Publishing, a division of ABDO, PO Box 398166, Minneapolis, MN 55439. Copyright © 2017 by Abdo Consulting Group, Inc. International copyrights reserved in all countries. No part of this book may be reproduced in any form without written permission from the publisher. Checkerboard Library™ is a trademark and logo of Abdo Publishing.

Printed in the United States of America, North Mankato, Minnesota.
062016
092016

Cover Photo: Shutterstock
Interior Photos: AP Images, p. 15; Shutterstock, pp. 1, 5, 7, 9, 11, 13, 16–17, 19, 21

Series Coordinator: Tamara L. Britton
Editor: Liz Salzmann
Production: Mighty Media, Inc.

Library of Congress Cataloging-in-Publication Data

Names: Polinsky, Paige V., author.
Title: Samoyeds / Paige V. Polinsky.
Description: Minneapolis, MN : Abdo Publishing, a division of ABDO, [2017] |
  Series: Dogs set 13 | Includes index.
Identifiers: LCCN 2016007823 (print) | LCCN 2016013320 (ebook) | ISBN
  9781680781793 (print) | ISBN 9781680775648 (ebook)
Subjects: LCSH: Samoyed dog--Juvenile literature. | Dog breeds--Juvenile
  literature.
Classification: LCC SF429.S35 P65 2016 (print) | LCC SF429.S35 (ebook) | DDC
  636.73--dc23
LC record available at http://lccn.loc.gov/2016007823

Contents

The Dog Family

Today's dogs come in many shapes and sizes. In fact, there are more than 400 **breeds** worldwide! But they are all members of the **Canidae** family. Coyotes, foxes, and wolves also belong to this family.

Scientists believe that dogs descended from wolves. Studies show that the Samoyed is more closely related to wolves than most other breeds. This is why it is one of 14 breeds considered "ancient."

Dogs and humans have worked together for thousands of years. The first **domesticated** dogs helped humans hunt. They also fought off predators and kept humans warm. In return, humans gave them food and shelter.

The Samoyed greatly resembles these early dogs. But it is friendlier than its ancestors. The Samoyed is an affectionate family dog with a rich history.

Samoyeds are closely related to the oldest domesticated dogs.

Samoyeds

Samoyeds originated hundreds of years ago in northwestern Siberia. They were important companions to the **nomadic** Samoyed people. The Samoyed people used these hardy dogs to pull heavy sleds and herd reindeer. The dogs slept with the Samoyed children to keep them warm. Their thick fur was even used to knit clothing!

Samoyed dogs were introduced to England around 1890. They became very popular and caught the attention of Queen Alexandra. She was soon an enthusiastic Samoyed supporter.

Belgian countess Rose de Mercy-Argenteau brought the first Samoyed to the United States in 1906. The dog had been a gift from a Russian duke. Later that year, the **American Kennel Club (AKC)** recognized the Samoyed as an official **breed**.

Many Samoyeds are still used in sled races and long-distance sledding.

The Samoyed quickly gained its reputation as a first-class sled dog. Explorers such as Roald Amundsen brought them on arctic expeditions. In 1911, one of Amundsen's Samoyeds led the first successful trip to the South Pole!

What They're Like

If you're searching for a loving companion, look no further than the Samoyed. This **breed** is known for its friendly, loyal personality. It's a real people pleaser and forms a tight bond with its family. These dogs are also very talkative! They often bark, howl, and sing.

The Samoyed is a big softie, both inside and out. It is excellent with children, strangers, and other pets. Its easygoing nature makes it a great family dog. And despite its stubborn streak, this breed responds well to training.

Similar to other working dogs, the Samoyed has energy to burn. It was bred to perform **intense** outdoor tasks. A bored Samoyed will try to make its own fun. This often means digging holes in the yard! Regular exercise and playtime generally keep this **breed** well behaved.

These friendly dogs are often called "smiling Sammies."

Coat and Color

The Samoyed is one of the fluffiest dogs you'll meet. Its **dense** double coat is designed for arctic winters. It has a long outer layer and a thick undercoat. A **ruff** of extra fur frames its head. Its heavy-duty coat lets the Samoyed endure temperatures as low as negative 60 degrees Fahrenheit (−51°C)!

Many recognize the Samoyed for its stunning white color. But not every Samoyed is white! The coat can also be **biscuit**, white and biscuit, or cream. Some Samoyeds have biscuit markings on their ears and around their eyes. No matter the coat's color, each hair has a shiny silver tip.

This **breed**'s cuddly coat comes at a cost. The Samoyed **sheds** heavily year-round. And twice a year, it sheds even more to remove its thick undercoat.

The Samoyed's coat allows it to easily shake off snow.

Size

The Samoyed is a blend of strength and grace. Adult males stand 21 to 23½ inches (53 to 60 cm) tall. They typically weigh 50 to 65 pounds (23 to 29 kg).

Adult female Samoyeds are slightly smaller. They measure 19 to 21 inches (48 to 53 cm) tall. On average, they weigh 35 to 50 pounds (16 to 23 kg).

This beautiful **breed** is muscular and big-boned. Its deep chest and strong neck are ideal for pulling heavy loads. It has powerful, moderately long legs. Its heavily furred tail curves upward over its back.

The Samoyed has a broad, wedge-shaped head and medium-length **muzzle**. Its triangular ears are erect and slightly rounded. This breed has bright, almond-shaped brown eyes. But the Samoyed is most famous for its charming, black-lipped smile.

The Samoyed is both powerful and elegant.

Care

The Samoyed needs a lot of grooming. You should brush your dog at least once a week. During its seasonal **shed**, this **breed** will need daily brushing. This will help keep your home fur free!

Your Samoyed's coat is great for cold weather. But too much heat can be dangerous. Keep your Samoyed cool and comfortable to avoid overheating.

Luckily, the Samoyed's thick fur stays quite clean on its own. You only need to wash it every few months. Trim your Samoyed's nails monthly, and check its ears for infection each week. Brush its teeth often for fresh breath and healthy gums.

The Samoyed is usually a sturdy dog. But conditions including blindness and **hip dysplasia** have been seen in the breed. Schedule your Samoyed

Washing a Samoyed's thick fur can take quite a while!

for regular checkups. A veterinarian can **spay** or **neuter** your dog. The vet can also give your Samoyed important **vaccinations**.

Feeding

Your Samoyed needs a balanced, high-protein diet to stay fit. Its **nutritional** needs depend on its size, age, and activity level. There are a variety of dry, wet, or semi-moist foods to choose from. Your vet can help determine what's right for your dog.

Feed your new puppy the same food its **breeder** gave it. This will help avoid an upset stomach. Your growing Samoyed pup should eat three meals each day. When it is an adult, feed it once or twice a day. Any changes to your Samoyed's diet should be made gradually.

Scheduled feeding times will help keep your Samoyed in shape.

It is also important for your Samoyed to always have fresh drinking water available. This will help prevent it from overheating.

Be careful not to overfeed a Samoyed. **Obesity** can make your dog more likely to get diseases such as **diabetes**. It can also lead to joint problems. Offer treats in moderation and watch your dog's weight. This will give it a longer, healthier life!

Things They Need

Your Samoyed was **bred** for the rugged outdoors. But it should live inside with you! This social breed likes to stick close to its family. It's happiest with a lot of love and attention. If left outside, a Samoyed should have a fenced-in yard with room to run.

There are a few important items your Samoyed will need. A roomy crate will give it a comfortable resting place. It will also help with **housebreaking**. And the Samoyed has been known to chew, especially when bored. So extra-sturdy food dishes and chew toys are a must!

Daily exercise is important for your Samoyed. This breed makes a great walking or jogging companion. It will need a leash, collar, and identification tags.

Training for dog sports is another great way to exercise your dog. The Samoyed shines at **agility**, herding, and weight-pulling. And don't forget winter activities! Your Samoyed will feel right at home sledding or snowshoeing with you.

A game of fetch is great exercise for your Samoyed.

Puppies

The average Samoyed **pregnancy** lasts 63 days. The mother then gives birth to a **litter** of five to seven puppies. These fluffy pups are blind and deaf at first. But they are able to see and hear after two weeks. After eight weeks, they can leave their mother.

If you are ready for a Samoyed, do some research. Choose a qualified **breeder** or shelter. Spend some time getting to know the puppy. Ask a lot of questions about its health and personality. Make sure it has been tested for common health problems.

Begin training your puppy right away. Be patient, but make it clear that you are the leader. Your Samoyed will respond best to short, positive training sessions. Introduce it to other people and animals. A healthy Samoyed will live for 12 to 14 years.

This fluffy little pup will become a strong, majestic adult.

Glossary

agility - a sport in which a handler leads a dog through an obstacle course during a timed race.

American Kennel Club (AKC) - an organization that studies and promotes interest in purebred dogs.

biscuit - a color that is a combination of light gray, yellow, and brown.

breed - a group of animals sharing the same ancestors and appearance. A breeder is a person who raises animals. Raising animals is often called breeding them.

Canidae (KAN-uh-dee) - the scientific Latin name for the dog family. Members of this family are called canids. They include wolves, jackals, foxes, coyotes, and domestic dogs.

dense - thick or compact.

diabetes - a disease in which the body cannot properly absorb normal amounts of sugar and starch.

domesticated - adapted to life with humans.

hip dysplasia (HIHP dihs-PLAY-zhuh) - unusual formation of the hip joint.

housebreak - to teach a dog to not go to the bathroom inside.

intense - marked by great energy, determination, or concentration.

litter - all of the puppies born at one time to a mother dog.

muzzle - an animal's nose and jaws.

neuter (NOO-tuhr) - to remove a male animal's reproductive glands.

nomadic - relating to a member of a group that moves from place to place.

nutritional - related to that which promotes growth, provides energy, repairs body tissues, and maintains life.

obesity - the condition of having too much body fat.

pregnancy - having one or more babies growing within the body.

ruff - long hair that grows on the neck of an animal.

shed - to cast off hair, feathers, skin, or other coverings or parts by a natural process.

spay - to remove a female animal's reproductive organs.

vaccination - a shot given to prevent illness or disease.

Websites

To learn more about Dogs, visit **booklinks.abdopublishing.com**. These links are routinely monitored and updated to provide the most current information available.

Index